wish

WRITTEN & COMPILED BY M.H. CLARK ✦ DESIGNED BY JILL LABIENIEC

COMPENDIUM
INCORPORATED

live inspired.

Right now is a perfect time.

This moment is the very beginning of all that is coming next. Right now there are possibilities all around you, bright and shining as stars, just waiting to be noticed. What would happen if you took a chance and pulled one of those possibilities a little closer?

Dream a dream that's bigger than you are. Hope for the things your heart wants most. Believe in the incredible. Go ahead. Make a wish. And watch what happens next.

It's the possibility of
having a dream come true that
makes life interesting.

PAULO COELHO

Believe in the fantastic, the miraculous, the unexpected.

That's the thing with magic. You've got to know it's still here, all around us, or it just stays invisible for you.

See the wondrous.
Welcome the impossible.

Believe there are no limits but the sky.

MIGUEL DE CERVANTES

See your own
unlimited potential.

...the sight of the stars makes me dream.

VINCENT VAN GOGH

Leave time for
moments of wonder.

We do not need magic to transform our world. We carry all of the power we need inside ourselves already.

J.K. ROWLING

Give yourself a chance
to prove what is possible.

You are never given a
wish without also being given
the power to make it true.

RICHARD BACH

Design your own future.
Write your own story.

We can do only what we think we can do.
We can be only what we think we can be.
We can have only what we think we can have.
What we do, what we are, what we have,
all depend upon what we think.

ROBERT COLLIER

Think great things.

The difficulties you meet will resolve themselves
as you advance. Proceed, and light will dawn and
shine with increasing clearness on your path.

JEAN LE ROND D'ALEMBERT

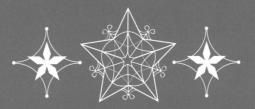

Keep faith, even in the dark.

Every great dream
begins with a dreamer.

HARRIET TUBMAN

Dream your dreams
in grand proportions.

Open your arms as wide as
you can to receive all the miracles
with your name on them.

SUZANNA THOMPSON

Accept all the
joys made just for you.

Listen to the MUSTN'TS, child. Listen
to the DON'TS. Listen to the SHOULDN'TS, the
IMPOSSIBLES, the WON'TS. Listen to the NEVER
HAVES, then listen close to me—anything can
happen, child, ANYTHING can be.

SHEL SILVERSTEIN

Keep your heart young
and your eyes wide.

Never give up. This may be your
moment for a miracle.

GREG ANDERSON

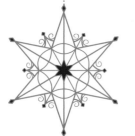

Welcome the extraordinary
in its own time.

Some things have to be believed to be seen.

RALPH HODGSON

Trust that you will find
what you seek.

Faith does for living what sunshine
does for stained-glass windows.

GERTA SCHAFFNER

Let belief light your life.

We are citizens of eternity.

FYODOR DOSTOYEVSKY

Make a wish that
will live on.

...I dream things that never were; and I say, "Why not?"

GEORGE BERNARD SHAW

Question limitations.

A possibility is a hint
from God. One must follow it.

SØREN KIERKEGAARD

Take opportunities when
they present themselves.

So many worlds, so much
to do, so little done, such things to be…

ALFRED LORD TENNYSON

Start today.

To accomplish great things,
we must not only act, but also dream;
not only plan, but also believe.

ANATOLE FRANCE

Believe with your head,
your heart, and your hands.

The most incredible thing about
miracles is that they happen.

G.K. CHESTERTON

Count all the wishes
already come true.

The human heart has hidden treasures…

CHARLOTTE BRONTË

Unlock your deep potential.
Listen to your soul.

I believe in the imagination. What I cannot
see is infinitely more important than what I can see.

DUANE MICHALS

Dream a greater
world into being.

I will love the light for it shows me
the way: yet I will love the darkness
for it shows me the stars.

OG MANDINO

Emphasize the good
of the present moment.

When you have exhausted all
possibilities, remember this—you haven't.

THOMAS EDISON

Give success
another chance.

There is a divine plan of
good at work in my life. I will
let go and let it unfold.

RUTH P. FREEDMAN

Trust in all the roads
you have yet to travel.

Dreams are renewable. No matter what our age
or condition, there are still untapped possibilities
within us and new beauty waiting to be born.

DALE TURNER

Be a lifelong dreamer.

Find the good. It's all around you. Find it,
showcase it, and you'll start believing in it.

JESSE OWENS

Play up the positive.

Let nothing dim the light
that shines from within.

MAYA ANGELOU

Give the best of yourself
to the world.

Look for heaven on Earth; it is all around you.

UNKNOWN

See beauty in the
here and now.

There wouldn't be a sky full of stars if
we were all meant to wish on the same one.

FRANCES CLARK

Wish your own secret wish.
Dream your own bright dream.

WITH SPECIAL THANKS TO THE ENTIRE COMPENDIUM FAMILY.

CREDITS
Written by: M.H. Clark
Designed by: Jill Labieniec
Edited by: Jennifer Pletsch
Creative Direction by: Sarah Forster

ISBN 978-1-935414-65-0

1st printing. Printed in China.